THE BLODGETT READERS

A PRIMER

BY

FRANCES E. BLODGETT

AND

ANDREW B. BLODGETT

SUPERINTENDENT OF SCHOOLS, SYRACUSE, N.Y.

BOSTON, U.S.A., AND LONDON
GINN & COMPANY, PUBLISHERS
The Athenæum Press

C

ENTERED AT STATIONERS' HALL

COPYRIGHT, 1904, BY
FRANCES E. BLODGETT AND ANDREW B. BLODGETT

ALL RIGHTS RESERVED

74.6

PREFACE

In the preparation of this Primer the aim has been to employ only such language as is familiar to children of the first school year. The stories are simple and natural. They touch every side of child life and closely connect the home and the school.

As the child recognizes these facts his pleasure in learning to read will increase and natural expression will readily follow.

The appendix contains brief suggestions to teachers, and a list of phonograms that apply particularly to all reading matter of this grade. The phonograms will be valuable aids in building up the vocabulary, and at the same time give the power necessary to the discovery of new words as the art of reading progresses.

Eleven hundred sentences have been prepared which introduce the new words in connection with each lesson. They are inclosed in fifty-five envelopes containing twenty sentences each.

We are confident that the simplicity of the language, the slow introduction of new words, the beautiful illustrations, and the attractive appearance of the pages will appeal to teacher and pupil alike.

THE AUTHORS.

THE BLODGETT PRIMER

see

my

my

my

See my

See my

2

I   a   this

I see a

I see a

See this

See this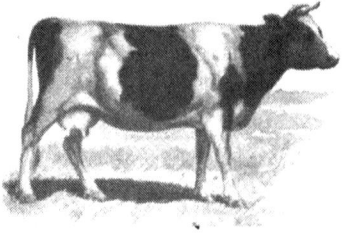

like   lit tle

I like my

I like my

I like my little

I like this

grand pa   is   pret ty   doll

This is my grandpa.
This is my doll.
I like my grandpa.
I like my pretty doll.

kit ty   name   Top sy   her

See this little kitty.
This is my kitty.
Her name is Topsy.
I like my little Topsy.

white　　Snow ball　　too　　black

This is a pretty kitty.
Her name is Snowball.
Snowball is a white kitty.
Topsy is a black kitty.
I like Topsy.
I like Snowball, too.

REVIEW

my	her	name
see	black	white
I	this	pretty
is	a doll	Topsy
like	kitty	little
grandpa	Snowball	too

See this black kitty.
Her name is Topsy.
Grandpa likes little black Topsy.
I like Snowball.
Snowball is my white kitty.
My little doll likes Snowball.
See my doll, grandpa.
This is a little doll.
I like my pretty little doll.
Topsy likes her, too.

the ball   have   you   ba by

I have a pretty ball.
The ball is black.
I like my little black ball.
Baby likes my ball.
Have you a ball?

moth er   dress   Ger trude   am

My name is Gertrude.
I am a little mother.
I have a pretty baby doll.
Her dress is white.
My dress is white.

bow wow   dog   Gyp   big

Bow wow! I am a big dog.
My name is Gyp.
I see a little black kitty.
Her name is Topsy.
Topsy is a baby kitty.
Snowball is her mother.
I have a mother, too.
Bow wow! Bow wow!

can   us   to run   he

See us run.
Gyp likes to run.
I like to run, too.
Have you a big dog?
Is he pretty like my Gyp?
Can he run like Gyp?

me   and   play   with

See my pretty dolls.
I like to play with my dolls.
Kitty and Gyp like to see me play.
This kitty is black and white.
Gyp likes to play with the kitty.
I like to play with her, too.
See my dolls and Gyp and kitty.

Gertrude   Gertrude's doll
doll   doll's dress
dog   dog's name
baby   baby's ball

This is Gertrude's doll.
The doll's dress is white.
Baby's dress is white, too.
This dog's name is Gyp.
My kitty's name is Snowball.
See Snowball play with baby's ball.

REVIEW WORDS

the ball	Gertrude	us	he
have	bow wow	can	to run
baby	dress	you	play
mother	dog	big	with
am	Gyp	and	me

REVIEW

I have a big dog.
He is a black and white dog.
He likes to play with us.
He likes to play with a ball.
My dog's name is Gyp.
Gyp likes Topsy and Snowball.
He runs with little Topsy.
He plays with pretty Snowball.
I like to see Gyp run and play.
Have you a big dog?
Can he run and play with you?
I like my dog and my kitty.
I like my pretty dolls.
I have a little baby doll.
I play I am her mother.
Have you a baby doll?

yel low   bird   sing   fly

I am a little yellow bird.
I can fly and fly.
I can sing, too.
I like to fly and sing.
Can you fly like a bird?
Can you sing?
Can you sing like me?

book   read   may   in

This is my book.
My book is a big book.
I can read in my book.
I can read to my little doll.
I can read to grandpa.
Grandpa likes my book.
You may read in my book, grandpa.
Read to me.

dan de li on   do   sun shine   grow

I am a big dandelion.
I have a pretty yellow dress.
See my baby dandelion.
Her dress is yellow, too.
I grow in the sunshine.
I like the sunshine.
Do you like me?

REVIEW

fly	in	do
sing	may	grow
bird	read	sunshine
yellow	book	dandelion

Do you see this yellow bird?
Can the little bird sing?
Can he fly?
Fly to me, little bird. I like you.
I like yellow dandelions, too.
Dandelions grow in the sunshine.
I play in the sunshine.
I play with my big ball.
Kitty plays with my ball, too.
I have a pretty book.
I can read in my book.
May I read and sing to you?

ride   rock ing-horse   Paul   on

My name is Paul.
See my little horse.
My horse is a rocking-horse.
See me ride on my horse.
Do you like to see me ride?
Have you a rocking-horse?
Can you ride on a rocking-horse?

want   his   Dan dy   not

This is grandpa's horse.
His name is Dandy.
Dandy is a black horse.
He can run.
My rocking-horse can not run.
I like Dandy, grandpa.
I like to see Dandy run.
I want to ride on Dandy.
I can ride. May I ride?

go   fast   whoa   here

Go on, Dandy. Run fast.
I like to ride fast.
See Dandy run.
Gyp can run fast, too.
Whoa! Dandy, whoa!
Gertrude wants me.
Here I am, Gertrude.
Do you want to ride?
You may ride. I can run with Gyp.
Do not go too fast, Dandy. Whoa!

tree   has   an ap ple   red

Here is an apple tree.
I am in the tree. Do you see me?
I play in this tree.
Gertrude plays with me.
My tree has pretty red apples.
Gertrude and I like red apples.

blue　　　three　　　are　　　they

I am a blue bird.
I have three baby birds.
They are blue, too.
My little birds can not sing.
They can not fly.
They are too little.
I can fly and sing.
I sing to my baby birds.
They are in the apple tree.
I like the big apple tree.

PICTURES TO FIND

find   pic ture   of   boy

1. Find a picture of a doll.
2. Find a picture of a dog.
3. Find a picture of a horse.
4. Find a picture of grandpa.
5. Find a picture of mother.
6. Find a picture of a baby.
7. Find a picture of Topsy.
8. Find a picture of a bird.
9. Find a picture of a tree.
10. Find a picture of Snowball.
11. Find a picture of a dandelion.
12. Find a picture of an apple.
13. Find a picture of a boy.
14. Find a picture of a book.
15. Find a picture of a rocking-horse.
16. Find a picture you like.

REVIEW

boy	go	has	rocking-horse
ride	not	they	Dandy
Paul	fast	red	an apple
want	on	find	three
blue	here	of	whoa
his	tree	are	picture

play	playing	ride	riding
sing	singing	go	going

MOTHER'S PICTURE BOOK

Mother has a picture book.
May I see the book, mother?
I like pretty pictures.
I like to find pictures in books.
Do you want to see pictures, grandpa?
See this picture of a tree.

Red apples grow on the tree.
A blue bird is in the tree.
He is singing to his baby birds.
Here is a picture of three dogs.
They are black dogs.
This is a picture of a kitty.
The kitty is playing with a ball.
See this picture of a rocking-horse.
A little boy is riding the horse.
Here is a picture of a dandelion.
I like big yellow dandelions.
You may have the book, grandpa.
I do not want to see pictures.
I want to go and find dandelions.
Paul, Paul, I want you.
I want you to go with me.
I am going to find dandelions.

Rose   home   nest   it

Here is a bird in my tree.
It is a mother bird.
I like the pretty birds.
The birds may have my tree.
A little nest is in the tree.
It is the birds' nest.
Do you see the nest, Rose?
See the mother bird fly to her nest.
The nest is her home.
Baby birds are in the nest.

fa ther   your   hear   come

The father bird is in the tree.
Hear the father bird sing.
Can you hear the father bird?
He sings to the mother bird.
He sings, "Come home, come home.
Your little birds want you."
See the mother bird fly home.
The little birds hear the father.
The little birds see the mother.
The baby birds can not sing.
The baby birds can not fly.

where   now   school   good

Run home, Gyp, run fast.
Do you hear me?
You are a good dog.
Go and play with baby.
I can not play with you now.
I am going to school.
Rose is going to school, too.
Rose, Rose, where are you?
Are you going to school with me?

REVIEW

Rose	father	where
home	your	now
nest	hear	school
it	come	good

fly   flying
come   coming

THE BOY AND THE BIRD

I hear you singing, little bird.
Are you in this tree?
Now I see you. Do not fly.
I want to hear you sing.
Is your nest in this tree?
I do not see your nest. Where is it?
I am going to school, little bird.

Can you fly to my school?
Fly, birdie, fly.
Do you hear me sing?
I can not sing like you.
I sing "Fly, Birdie, Fly" in school.
Here is Gyp, little bird.
Gyp is my dog.
He is coming to find me.
Come here, Gyp.
Come and see this pretty bird.
It is a blue bird.
Sing, little bird, sing to Gyp and me.
The bird can not sing now.
He is going to see his baby birds.
See, he is flying to his nest.
I am going to school, Gyp.
I do not want you.
Dogs do not go to school.
Go home like a good dog.

Fred draw for she

Here are Fred and Rose.
See Fred draw.
He is drawing a picture for Rose.
Rose likes Fred's pictures.
She can not draw.
She likes to see Fred draw.
Can you draw pictures?
Do you draw in your school?
Can you draw a picture like this?

girl		kit tens		milk		four

I am a little girl.
I have four pretty kittens.
Do you see my pretty kittens?
They are going with me.
I am going for milk.
The milk is for the kittens.
Have you a little kitty?
Is she a black and white kitty?
Can she run and play with you?

some   mouse   did   catch

Run fast, little mouse. Kitty is here.
I do not want the kitty to catch you.
Have you a nest, little mouse?
Where is your nest?
Where is your mother?
Run to your nest and your mother.
Come here, you little black kitty.
Here is some milk for you.
You did not see the mouse, did you?

will　　　give　　　drink　　　thank

Here are four little dogs.
See the boy give the dogs some milk.
See the dogs drink the milk.
They like milk.
Some dogs do not like milk.
My dog will not drink it.
My kitten and I like milk.
Will you give us a drink, big boy?
Thank you. I like you.

Gyp likes to r–n.
The kittens run and pl–y.
Hear the blue birds s–ng.
See the pretty n–st in the tree.
Gertrude has a big d–ll.
Her doll has a pretty wh–te dress.
My doll has a bl–e dress.
I go to sch– –l.
I can r– –d in my book.
Fred can dr–w a picture.
He will g–ve you a picture.
Paul r–des on grandpa's horse.
The horse is a bl–ck horse.
See the little m– –se run.
The kitten will not c–tch the mouse.
Some apples are y–llow.
Some apples are r–d.
A dandelion has a yellow dr–ss.
Boys and girls l–ke dandelions.

REVIEW

Fred	girl	some	will
draw	kittens	mouse	give
for	milk	did	drink
she	four	catch	thank

DRAWING PICTURES

I am going to draw some pictures.
Where are my kittens?
Come here, Snowball and Topsy.
Do not run and play.
I want to draw your picture.
I will give your picture to Rose.
She will like it.
See, Fred, see my picture of the kittens.
Is it a good picture?
Come, Snowball! Come, Topsy!
Now I will give you some milk.

You are good kittens.
You may have a drink of milk.
Can you draw a picture of Gyp, Fred?
I will go and find Gyp for you.
Here, Gyp, come here. Fred wants you.
He is going to draw your picture.
Can you draw a bird, Fred?
Draw four birds in an apple tree.
I will draw a doll for Gertrude.
She likes dolls.
I will draw a mouse, too.
And I will draw a horse.
See my picture of a horse.
I will give it to father.
Did you draw some birds, Fred?
Give your pictures to mother.
Father and mother like pictures.

hen			Cac kle			old			eggs

This is Cackle and I.
Cackle is grandpa's old hen.
I can run and catch her.
I can play with her.
She is a good old hen.
She likes to play with me.
Some hens do not like to play.
Cackle has a big nest.
You can not find her nest.
I do not want you to find it.
I can find it.
I find eggs in Cackle's nest.
I give the eggs to grandpa.
Have you a hen to play with?
Can you find her nest?
Is she a good old hen?
Can she play like Cackle?

what   Bess   feed   cow

This is grandpa's white cow.
Her name is Bess.
She gives good milk.
See grandpa milk old Bess.
I can not milk a cow.
I can feed a cow.
I feed apples to old Bess.
She likes red and yellow apples.
I like to see you milk, grandpa.
What will you do with the milk?
May baby and I have a drink?
Thank you, Bess, for your good milk.

farm corn house one

Grandpa has a big farm.
He has a big house, too.
The house is a farmhouse.
Grandpa has hens on his farm.
He has horses and cows.
Rose and I like to go to the farm.
I ride on the horses.
Gyp and I go for the cows.
Rose feeds the hens. They like her.
One is a big black hen.
It is Cackle. She runs to Rose.
Rose feeds her corn. Hens like corn.
Grandpa's hens have a house.
Have your hens a house, too?
Do you like hens?
Do you like cows and horses?
Can you ride on a horse?

look at how many

Look at this picture.
What do you see in the picture?
How many cows do you see?
How many horses do you see?
How many black cows do you see?
How many white horses do you see?
Do you see the hens?
What can hens do for us?
What can cows do for us?
What can horses do for us?

REVIEW

hen	what	farm	look
Cackle	Bess	corn	at
old	feed	house	how
eggs	cow	one	many
	do	doing	
	run	running	

FRED ON THE FARM

Gyp, Gyp, where are you?
I am going for the cows.
Do you want to go with me?
What a big farm my grandpa has!
See, Gyp, how many trees he has!
Hear the birds sing in the trees.
Hear the hens cackle.
I am going to feed the hens.

Where is my old black hen?
What is she doing?
Gyp, Gyp, come here.
See this nest in the henhouse.
It is Cackle's nest.
Look at the eggs in the nest.
Here comes Cackle.
She is running fast.
How do you do, old hen?
You have four eggs in your nest.
May I have three eggs?
Here is some corn.
Do you want it?
Give me the eggs and I will give you the corn.

Thank you, you are a good hen.
I will give the eggs to my mother.
Come, Gyp, grandpa will want to milk the cows.

oh   cart .   yes   new

Father wants you, Paul.
Yes, Gertrude, I am coming.
Where is father? Is he in the house?
Oh, here you are, father.
Did you want me?
Yes, Paul; see this new cart.
It is for you. Do you like it?
Yes, I do. Thank you, father.
I can not ride in it, can I?
It is a little cart and I am a big boy.
How can I play with it?
Oh, Gertrude's dolls can ride in it.
The kittens can ride in it, too.
I can play Gyp is the horse.
He can draw the cart.
Where is Gyp, Gertrude?
Find Gyp and the kittens.

we   rains   um brel la   our

Oh! oh! oh! see how it rains!
We are going to school.
We like to go to school in the rain.
We are big boys and girls.
Look at our umbrellas.
How many do you see?
Mother has a sun umbrella.
Ours are for the rain.
Have you an umbrella?
Do you go to school in the rain?
Run fast, Paul.
I can see our schoolhouse.

must　　　day　　　glad　　　kite

Look! Rose, look! See my kite fly.
Where is it going?
I must run fast.
I am glad the sun shines.
This is a good day to fly my kite.
It will not fly in the rain.
Can you fly a kite, Rose?
You must run fast like this.
Now see where the kite will go.

Rob ert   flag   drum   sol dier

Is this your new flag, Robert?
What a big flag it is!
Did your father give it to you?
My father will give me one some day.
Here is my new drum.
How do you like it?
We have my drum and your flag to play with.
Now we can play soldier.
How do you play soldier, Fred?
What do soldiers do?

What is Rose doing?
Rose is feeding the hens.
What is Gertrude doing?
She is playing with her doll.
What is mother doing?
She is singing to baby.
What is Fred doing?
Fred is drawing a picture.
What is father doing?
He is reading a book.
What is Paul doing?
He is catching the ball.
What are the birds doing?
The birds are flying to the nest.
What are the kittens doing?
They are drinking some milk.
What is the little mouse doing?
He is running to his nest.
What are you doing?

gave   Daisy
to-day   hair

How do you do, girls?
Have you come to see my new doll?
Here she is. How do you like her?
Mother gave her to me to-day.
See her yellow hair.
I am glad she has yellow hair.

My hair is black like yours.

How do you like her dress?

I am going to name this doll Daisy.

Now, Daisy, you must be a good little girl.

I am your mother.

I am a good mother.

Do you want to play with Daisy, Rose?

I have three old dolls.

We will play with the old dolls, too.

REVIEW WORDS

oh	yes	kite	umbrella
new	we	day	Robert
rains	flag	gave	Daisy
cart	our	hair	soldier
glad	must	drum	to-day

REVIEW

have not   have n't   can not   can't
is not   is n't   do not   don't

BOYS AT PLAY

Oh, here you are, Robert.
I am glad you have come.
Now what can we play to-day?
Oh, we can fly our kites.
We can play ball, too.
This is my new ball, Robert.
Fred gave it to me.
Fred has three big balls.
How many have you?
Now you must see my cart.
It is in the house.
I will go and find it.
Here it is. Do you like it?

I am glad father gave me a red cart.
Red carts are pretty.
Gyp can draw my cart.
Do you want to see Gyp draw it?
O Robert, look! It is raining.
We can not fly our kites now.
We can not play ball.
We must go into the house.
What can we do in the house?
Do you want to play soldier?
I will run and find my drum.
I don't see your flag.
Your flag isn't here.
We can't play soldier.
We haven't a flag.
Do you want to read?
Oh! oh! see the sunshine.
How glad I am! Now we can play.

Thanks giv ing gob ble tur keys a way

Gobble gobble!
Look at this boy, my baby turkeys.
Look at this girl.
Thanksgiving day is coming.
Gobble gobble!
Boys and girls like Thanksgiving.
I do not like Thanksgiving.
I do not like boys and girls.
Gobble gobble! Gobble gobble!
This boy is Fred.
He comes to see us on the farm.
He likes to feed us corn.
He likes big turkeys.
He will come to catch us some day.
I do not want the boy to catch us.
What can we do?
Where can we go?
We will run away.
The boy can not find us.

seen   says   help   know

Run away, Gyp. I can not play to-day.
Mother says I must help her.
I am glad I can help my mother.
You can't help, Gyp.
You don't know how to help.
Have you seen my big new doll?
Go and play with her.
Mother and I don't want you now.
Some day I will play with you.

flow ers　　　two　　　be　　　why

See how many flowers we have.
They are for mother.
How glad she will be!
Mother likes pretty flowers.
Oh, here are two yellow flowers.
Are they roses? Father likes roses.
We will give the roses to father.
Mother says flowers like the rain.
Why do flowers like the rain?

cake　　birth day　　can dles　　par ty

To-day is my birthday.

This is my birthday party.

Gertrude and her dolls have come to my party.

Mother says I am a big girl now.

I am glad I am a big girl.

Do you want to know how old I am?
Look at my pretty birthday cake.
Do you see some little candles?
How many candles do you see?
One, two, three, four.
Now you know how old I am.
See how many dolls are here.
The three big dolls are my dolls.
The four little dolls are Gertrude's.
Daisy is the doll with yellow hair.
Do you see her?
Here is some milk, Gertrude.
And here is some cake.
What good cake this is!
Oh, see my little black kitty.
She has come to my party, too.
I am glad to see you, little kitty.
Here is a drink of milk for you.
Some day you may have a party.

REVIEW

Thanksgiving	gobble	know	two
flowers	seen	why	be
birthday	away	help	cake
candles	turkeys	says	party

MOTHER'S BIRTHDAY

This is my mother's birthday.
She is going to have a party.
Will you come to the party, Robert?
Mother will be glad to see you.
Look at this big white cake.
It is mother's birthday cake.

Father says we must have some candles.

Grandpa will give us some flowers.
How good grandpa is!

He gave me flowers on my birthday.
He gave us a turkey, too.
Father will give mother a book.
What can you give her, Fred?
Can you draw her a picture?
Draw a picture of a bird's nest.
Draw four little eggs in the nest.
I will help you draw it.
Paul has a new umbrella for mother.
Have you seen it? Here it is.
Isn't it a pretty umbrella?
I will give mother one of my kittens.
Rose will give her a kitten, too.
Oh, we like birthdays at our house.
Father plays he is a little boy.
He helps Paul fly his kite.
He plays soldier with Fred.
He reads mother's book to us.
What do you do on your birthday?

gar den   toad   would   hop

How do you do, little toad?
I am glad to see you.
What are you doing here?
Would you like to go with me?
Come, hop into my cart.
I will give you a ride in the garden.
I am going to help my mother.
She is in the garden with her flowers.
Her flowers want a drink.
Would you like a drink, too?

love   no   but   who

I help you, little boys and girls.
I read to you. I sing to you.
I give you pretty books and carts.
I say "Yes" and "No" to you.
I love you and you love me.

Who am I?

I do not see. I do not run.
I do not fly. I do not play.
I do not sing. I do not read.
I do not go to school.
But little girls love me.

What am I?

lives   Ruth   beau ti ful   rob ins

This little girl's name is Ruth.
Ruth lives in this pretty house.
She has three dolls and two kittens.
She gives her kittens milk.

Ruth plays in this beautiful garden.
The kittens play here, too.
Do you see the flowers in the garden?
Do you see the beautiful trees?
Little robins live in the trees.
Ruth likes to hear the robins sing.
She likes to hear her mother sing, too.
This is what Ruth's mother sings:

    Up, up in the sky,
      The little birds fly.
    Down, down in the nest,
      The little birds rest.

    With a wing on the left,
      And a wing on the right,
    The dear little birds
      Sleep all the long night.

sand　　　make　　　them　　　tell

How white this sand is!
I like to play in it.
I will make a big house now.
This house will be for our big dolls.
Can you make some sand cakes, Rose?
Dolls like sand cakes.
How many houses have we now?
One, two, three. We have three houses.
Now we will make a pretty garden.
Oh! We must have trees in our garden.
We must have some flowers, too.
Where can we find them?
Mother will tell us.
She will help us make a garden.

dai sies field all hap py

Oh, you pretty flowers!
I am glad to see you.
What is your name?
We are daisies, little girl.
Don't you know us?
Why, my doll's name is Daisy, too.

Do you live here, little daisies?
Yes, we live in this beautiful field.
We are happy little flowers.
What do you do all day?
You can not play, can you?
Oh, yes; we play with the yellow dandelions.
They grow here in the field.
Don't you see them?
Yes, I see the dandelions.
But can you tell me what makes you grow?
The sun and the rain make us grow.
We want to be big daisies.
We love the sun and the rain.

John ny　　spi der　　Mrs.　　cob web

Look, Johnny! Look, baby! What is this?

Why, it is a big black spider!

What is she doing here?

Oh, see how fast she runs!

Do not run away, Mrs. Spider.

We will not catch you.
We want to see what you are doing.
Oh, I know what she is doing, Johnny.
Mrs. Spider is making a cobweb.
Isn't it beautiful?
Why is she making a cobweb?
Is this Mrs. Spider's house?
Is she going to live here?
How do spiders make cobwebs?

"Will you walk into my parlor?"
   Said the spider to the fly;
"It is the prettiest parlor
   That ever you did spy.
The way into my parlor
   Is up a winding stair,
And I have many pretty things
   To show when you are there."

REVIEW

Tell us a little girl's name.
Tell us a little boy's name.
Tell us your doll's name.
Tell us your kitty's name.
Tell us the name of some one you love.
Who can tell the name of a tree?
Who can tell the name of a flower?
Who can tell the name of a bird?
Tell what the little bird makes.
Tell what the little spider makes.
Tell us what you can make.
Tell us where the little birds live.
Tell us where the flowers live.
Tell us where you live.
Tell us why you go to school.
Tell us why the flowers love the rain.
Tell us why they love the sunshine.

Do you help your mother?
What do you do to help her?
Do you sing in school?
What do you like to sing?
What do you like to read?
What do you like to play?
Can you draw a picture of your doll?
Can you draw a picture of your kitty?
How many dolls and kittens have you?
Has your grandpa a farm?
Where is the farm?
Do you go to the farm?
Do you feed the hens and turkeys?
What do you feed the cows?
Do you find eggs in the hens' nests?
What do you like to do?
What do you want to be?

left   right   foot   march

We are playing soldier.
Now we are going to march.
This is the left foot.
This is the right foot.
Left foot! right foot! left foot! right foot! One, two, three, march!
Left, right, left, right, left, right.
We are marching like soldiers.

cap tain   by   hur rah   cheer

I am the captain.
I tell the boys what to do.
The boys are good soldiers.
They do what I say.
The boy with the flag is Robert.
See how his flag is flying.
Paul has the drum.
Do you know what Fred has?
We have marched by the fields.

Now we are marching by our schoolhouse.

We have a new flag on our schoolhouse.

It is red, white, and blue.
We love our beautiful flag.
Cheer, boys; cheer the flag!
Hurrah for the red, white, and blue!

swing   un der   Mr.   ev er

Fred, come here. I am in the swing.
Come and swing with me.

I like to play under this big tree.
Mr. Robin likes to play here, too.
He and Mrs. Robin live in this tree.
They like to have me come here.
They do not fly away.
Some days I feed them cake.
They are happy birds.
They have some baby birds in the nest.

Did you ever see a bird's nest, Fred?
Why, here is Robin now!
How do you do, Mr. Robin?
How is Mrs. Robin?
Do your baby birds grow?
See Robin hop in the sand, Fred.
He hops like a little toad.
He is looking for cake.

We have no cake for you to-day, Mr. Robin.

so   let   went   said

One day father said, "Come, boys and girls.

"I have a beautiful new book.

"Who would like to see the book?"

Fred said, "O father! I want to see it."

Paul said, "I want to see it, too."

Gertrude and Rose said, "We all want to see it." So father said:

"Let us go into the garden.

"We will look at the book under the apple tree."

So they all went with father into the garden.

bear

Billy

woods

shall

"Now we will look at the book," said father.

"We will look at the pictures.

"Here in the woods is a little black ----."

"Oh, I know what it is!" said Fred.

"So do I," said Paul.

"I know, too," said Gertrude.

"Let me tell what it is, father," said Rose.

"It is a little black bear.

"Shall I tell you what his name is?

"His name is Billy Bear."

was　　　had　　　wher ev er　　　fun ny

Father did not know Rose had seen a bear.

So he said, "Why, Rose!

"How do you know this is a bear?

"Have you ever seen one?"

"No, father, I have not seen a bear.

"But I have seen Billy's picture.

"Mother has it.

"She says Billy lived in the woods.

"He went with his mother wherever she went.

"He was a funny little bear."

"O father! tell us what Billy did," said Paul.

So father read a little in the book.

"Here is a funny picture of Billy.

"He is in a tree," said father.

"He is looking at his mother.

"She is under the tree.

"Billy did not grow to be a big bear.

"Fred can read the book to you.

"I must go now."

get   me ow   if   hun gry

Meow! meow! meow! Hear us sing.
We are all so happy.
We are having a party.
To-day is little Topsy's birthday.
The sun shines. It will not rain.
We can play all day under this tree.
See this swing, my baby kittens.
You may all swing.

Now, Snowball, go and get some milk.

Run fast. We are hungry.

I will make a big white cake.

Boys and girls have birthday cakes.

We must have a cake, too.

You may help me, Topsy.

Run and get some candles.

Your cake must have some candles.

We must have flowers, too, for our party.

I will go and find some daisies.

Now you little kittens may run and play.

You may sing, too, if you like.

No one will hear you in this field.

No one will see you.

No one will say, "Run away, little kitty."

REVIEW

A DAY IN THE WOODS

Hurrah! We are going to the woods.
Father is going with us.
How happy we are!
It is a beautiful day.
Get your flag and drum, boys.
We will play soldier in the woods.
And father says he will make us a swing.
Oh, see this field of daisies!
I like daisies.
Here is a big cobweb on this daisy.
Run away, Mrs. Spider.
You must not make your house here.
Do daisies ever grow in a garden, father?

Dandelions grow in our garden.
Hear the robins sing.
They are happy, too.
May we have our swing under your tree, Mrs. Robin?

May we see the blue eggs in your nest?

Here we are in the woods.

Now, father, shall we play soldier?

You may be the captain and tell us what to do.

Would you like to see us march?

We know how to march.

Left foot! right foot! left foot! right foot!

Let us cheer the flag, boys.

Cheer now; give a good cheer.

One, two, three. Hurrah!

Hurrah for the red, white, and blue!

How hungry I am!

I am going to see if I can find an apple.

Do apple trees grow in the woods?

O Robert, look! look!

See what father has.

He has some little cakes.

Where did you get them, father?

Did mother give them to you?

Mother knows what we like.

See, father has a book, too.

He is going to read to us by and by.

Maybe it is the " Billy Bear" book.

Do bears live in the woods now?

Grandpa went to see a bear one day.

He said the bear was a big white bear.

Did you ever see a white bear, father?

eat ducks wa ter cold

How do you do, little girl?
Do you know what we are?
I will tell you. We are ducks.
We live in this pretty garden.
Do you see this beautiful water?
We live on the water, too.
We like to play on the water.
We are glad we are ducks.
We are cold and hungry now.
We want some corn to eat.
Will you give us some corn?

holes　　squir rels　　nuts　　win ter

O Robert, do look!
Here are two big squirrels.
What are they doing in this tree?
Let us go under the tree and see.

No, Ruth, don't go under the tree.

The squirrels will see us and run away.

How funny they look, Robert!

Can you see what they are doing?

Yes, Ruth, they are eating nuts.

Do squirrels live in the trees?

Yes, some of them live in holes in the trees.

Do they live here in the winter, too?

Yes, they make a nest in a hole in a tree.

They live in the nest all winter.

I want to see a squirrel's nest.

How do they make it, Robert?

Is it like a bird's nest?

bas ket　　car ry　　think　　out

See my pretty new basket, Gertrude.
What do you think I have in my basket?
I don't know. Is it a kitten, Ruth?
No, it is not a kitten.
Maybe you have an apple.
No, it is not an apple.
I can't think what you have.
May I look into the basket and see?
O Ruth! you have some nuts.
What are you going to do with them?
They are for the squirrels, Gertrude.
Squirrels like to eat nuts, you know.
Winter is coming by and by.
They can not find nuts in the winter.

Here is the squirrels' tree.

Do you think they are at home?

Maybe they are out looking for nuts.

I will carry my basket under the tree.

Now we will run away.

By and by the squirrels will come home.

Mr. Squirrel will see the basket.

He will say, "Oh my! look at this basket of nuts."

Mrs. Squirrel will look and run into the hole.

She will tell the baby squirrels.

They will all come out to see.

Mrs. Squirrel will say, "I think some little girl wants to help us.

"How glad I am!

"Now we shall have nuts all winter."

sled   please   that   hel lo

Winter has come. Hurrah! hurrah! Now we can make snowballs and play with our sleds.

Hello, Fred! is that your new sled?

Let me see it, please.

What a big sled it is!

Where did you get it?

Will you please give me a ride?

How white the snow is and how fast we go!

I like to ride with you on your big new sled.

SOMETHING FOR YOU TO DO

1. You may get me a drink of water.
2. You may give the flowers a drink.
3. You may find a basket.
4. You may look into the basket.
5. You may give some one an apple.
6. You may eat an apple.
7. You may carry the basket away.
8. You may sing for us.
9. You may read to us.
10. You may find a picture you like.
11. You may give me your book.
12. You may draw a mouse.
13. You may draw a kite.
14. You may draw a bird in a tree.
15. You may get the flags.
16. You may play you are soldiers.
17. You may march in twos.

REVIEW

THE NEW BOOK

I have a new book, Robert.

You must see it.

My father gave it to me.

The name of the book is "Mr. Squirrel at Home."

Father said, "To-day is your birthday, Fred.

"What shall I give you?"

I said, "O father! I want a new book, if you please."

He said, "All right; you may have it."
Isn't he a good father?
He gave me my sled, too.
I did not know he was going to do that.
Let us look at the book, Robert.
How many beautiful pictures it has!
Here is the tree where the squirrels live.
Here is the hole where the nest is.
I am glad I am not a squirrel.
They must be cold in the winter.
In this picture Mr. Squirrel is eating nuts.
Here he is carrying nuts to his nest.
This must be Mrs. Squirrel.
See, she is helping him carry nuts.
Maybe they have some baby squirrels in the nest.

Maybe the baby squirrels are hungry.
Isn't it funny to see them carry nuts?
I am glad I know how they do it.

I said, "Father, how do squirrels carry nuts?

"They can not carry them in baskets."

Father said, "Read your book.

"It will tell you."

So I read my book and now I know.

Do you think the birds know the squirrels?

They live in the trees with them.

Do they fly away if they see a squirrel?

They do fly if they see my kitten.
Hello, Johnny! is that you?
Do you want to see my new book?
Robert and I are going out to play now.

O Robert! let us go to see Fred White. He has four black ducks.

What do you think of that?

Did you ever see a black duck?

Maybe they will be out on the water.

We will carry them some corn.

If they are at home, we will feed them.

can dy   Christ mas   for get
San ta Claus

Hello, Santa Claus! Is that you?
Can you hear what I say?

I am a little girl. My name is Rose.

I am glad Christmas is coming, Santa Claus.

Are you coming to our house on Christmas?

What is that you say, Santa?

You would like to know if I am a good girl?

Why, yes, I think so.

Father says I am his good little girl.

May I tell you what I want for Christmas?

Now, Santa Claus, please give me a doll with yellow hair.

Have you ever seen Ruth's doll?

I want one like hers.

The doll must have some dresses, you know.

One red dress and three white dresses will do.

Oh! I think she must have a blue dress, too.

And, Santa, please give me a sled like Fred's.

The sled must have my name on it.

R-O-S-E is my name.

Did you hear, Santa Claus?

I want a new book, too, if you please, and a basket to carry flowers in.

Oh! and I like candy and nuts.

All girls and boys like candy, don't they?

I think that is all, thank you.

Don't forget to come, Santa Claus. Good-by.

THE ALPHABET

A a	B b	C c	D d
E e	F f	G g	H h
I i	J j	K k	L l
M m	N n	O o	P p
Q q	R r	S s	T t
U u	V v	W w	X x
	Y y		Z z

1 2 3 4 5 6 7 8 9 0

APPENDIX

GUIDE TO PRONUNCIATION

A key to the diacritical markings used in the word list.

I. VOWELS

ā	as in	fāte	ė	as in	ėvent	ō	as in	ōbey
ȧ	"	senȧte	ĕ	"	mĕt	ŏ	"	nŏt
ă	"	făt	ẽ	"	hẽr	ōō	"	fōod
ä	"	ärm	ī	"	īce	ŏŏ	"	fŏot
a̤	"	a̤ll	ĭ	"	ĭdea	ū	"	ūse
ȧ	"	ȧsk	ĭ	"	ĭt	u̇	"	u̇nite
â	"	câre	ĩ	"	sĩr	ŭ	"	ŭp
ē	"	mēte	ō	"	ōld	û	"	fûr

II. EQUIVALENTS

a̤ = ŏ	as in	wha̤t	o̭ = ōō	as in	wo̭lf	u̬ = ōō	as in	pu̬ll
ê = â	"	thêre	ȯ = ŭ	"	sȯn	ȳ = ī	"	flȳ
ĩ = ẽ	"	gĩrl	ô = a̤	"	hôrse	y̆ = ĭ	"	baby̆
o̱ = ōō	"	mo̱ve	u̱ = ōō	"	ru̱le			

III. CONSONANTS

ç = s	as in	miçe	th	as in thĕm
c or c (unmarked) = k			th (unmarked)	" thin
	as in	ca̤ll	ph = f	" phantom
ch = k	"	schōol	s̱ = z	" ĭs̱
ch (unmarked)	"	child	z (like s sonant)	" zone
ġ like j	"	cāġe	qu (unmarked)	" quite
ḡ (hard)	"	ḡĕt	x̱ = gz	" ex̱act
n̠ = ng	"	ĭn̠k	x (unmarked) = ks	" vex

SOUNDS OF THE LETTERS

VOWELS

At this early stage of learning to read, the diacritical markings of the long and short vowels alone should be used and these in blackboard and drill work only. The short sounds, ă, ĕ, ĭ, ŏ, ŭ, should be taught some weeks before the long sounds, ā, ē, ī, ō, ū, as the latter introduce the troublesome silent letter.

CONSONANTS

Each consonant *says* something and *is* something, and the difference between what each *says* and *is* should be clearly taught. To this end teach the sound (what it says) and the alphabetic name (what it is) of each consonant clearly; the *sound* being taught some time in advance of the *name*. This can best be accomplished by the use of cards as suggested in the teaching of phonograms.

PHONOGRAMS

The following phonograms will be found adapted to the reading matter in this book, and as the words are frequently repeated in this and succeeding books, it is desirable that the children should be familiar with them and be able to pronounce them at sight. Many others may be added at the pleasure of the teacher as the children take up supplementary reading.

It is suggested that teachers make up a set of cards containing these phonograms for the first year's work. This can easily be done by using heavy manila paper, 6 by 8 inches, and printing one phonogram in large type on each slip. Teach and review these frequently by exposing them in plain view of each member of the class. Make it a quick exercise for the entire class.

This exercise, or drill, will give the children power to recognize new words as the reading progresses, and will produce the confidence and mastery so essential to rapid progress.

it	ig	ap	orn
an	un	ed	ook
and	ay	ind	art
ame	in	est	ust
op	ing	ill	ad
ite	ine	ilk	ob
aw	ide	id	ake
et	ock	atch	ag
ack	oy	ink	ut
ess	ot	ank	ight
ell	ast	en	ent
am	at	arm	old

WORD LIST

The following is a list of the words used in this Primer, arranged by pages, in the order of their appearance.

PAGE 1
sēe
mȳ

2
I
ā
thĭs

3
līke
lĭt'tle

4
grănd'pä
ĭs̩
pretty
(prĭt'tў)
dŏll

5
kĭt'tў
nāme
Tŏp'sў
hĕr

6
whīte
Snōw'ball

tо̭о̭
blăck

8
thē
ball
hăve
bā'bў
you

9
mȯth'ĕr
drĕss
Gertrude
(ĝĕr'trу̭d)
ăm

10
bow'wow
dŏḡ
Ġўp
bĭḡ

11
eăn
ŭs
tо̭

rŭn
hē

12
mē
ănd
plāy
wĭth

15
yĕl'lŏw
bĭrd
sĭng
flȳ

16
bo͝ok
rēad
māy
ĭn

17
dăn'dė līȯn
do̭
sŭn'shīne
grōw

19
rīde
rŏck'ĭng-hôrse
Paul
(pa̩l)
ŏn

20
wa̩nt
hĭs̩
Dăn'dў
nŏt

21
ḡо̄
fȧst
whōa
hēre

22
trēe
hăs̩
ăn
ăp'ple
rĕd

110

23
blūe
thrēe
äre
they (thā)

24
fĭnd
pĭc′tŭre
of (ŏv)
boy

28
Rōṣe
hōme
nĕst
ĭt

29
fä′thĕr
your
hēar
come

30
whêre
now
schōōl
gōŏd

33
Frĕd
draw
fôr
shē

34
gīrl
kĭt′tens̩
mĭlk
fōur

35
sȯme
mouse
dĭd
cătch

36
wĭll
gīve
drĭnk
thănk

41
hĕn
Căc′kle
ōld
ĕggs̩

42
what
Bĕss
fēed
cow

43
färm
côrn
house
one (wŭn)

44
lŏŏk
ăt
how
many (mĕn′y̆)

47
ōh
cärt
yĕs
new (nū)

48
wē
rāins̩

ŭm brĕl′lȧ
our

49
mŭst
dāy
glăd
kīte

50
Rŏb′ĕrt
flăg
drŭm
soldier (sōl′jĕr)

52
gāve
Dāi′s̩y̆
to-dāy′
hâir

56
Thănks gĭv′ĭng
gŏb′ble
tûr′key̆s̩
ȧ wāy′

58
sēen
says (sĕs)

hĕlp
knōw

59
flow'ĕrṣ
twọ
bē
whȳ

60
cāke
bîrth'dăy
căn'dleṣ
pär'tў

64
ḡär'den
tōad
wọuld
hŏp

65
lóve
nō
bŭt
whọ

66
lĭveṣ
Rūth
beaū'tĭ fụl
rŏb'ĭnṣ

69
sănd
māke
thĕm
tĕll

70
dā*i*'ṣĭeṣ
fīeld
ạll
hăp'pў

72
Jŏhn'nў
spī'dĕr
Mrs.
cŏb'wĕb

76
lĕft
rīg*h*t
foot
märch

77
căp'ta*i*n
bȳ
hụr rä*h*'
chēer

78
swĭng
ŭn'dĕr
Mr.
ĕv'ĕr

80
sō
lĕt
wĕnt
said
(sĕd)

81
beâr
Bĭl'lў
wŏŏdṣ
shăll

82
waṣ
hặd
whêr ĕv'ĕr
fŭn'nў

84
ḡĕt
meow
(mē ou')
ĭf
hŭn̄'grў

89
ēat
dŭcks
wạ'tĕr
cōld

90
hōleṣ
squir'rĕlṣ
nŭtṣ
wĭn'tĕr

92
bȧs'kĕt
câr'rў
thĭnk
out

94
slĕd
pleaṣe
thạt
hĕl lō'

100
Săn'tȧ Claụṣ
căn'dў
Christ'mas
fŏr ḡĕt'

112

ALPHABETIC LIST OF WORDS USED

a	bowwow	dandelion	flowers
all	boy	Dandy	fly
am	but	day	foot
an	by	did	for
and		do	forget
apple	Cackle	dog	four
are	cake	doll	Fred
at	can	draw	funny
away	candles	dress	
	candy	drink	garden
baby	captain	drum	gave
ball	carry	ducks	Gertrude
basket	cart		get
be	catch	eat	girl
bear	cheer	eggs	give
beautiful	Christmas	ever	glad
Bess	cobweb		go
big	cold	farm	gobble
Billy	come	fast	good
bird	corn	father	grandpa
birthday	cow	feed	grow
black		field	Gyp
blue	daisies	find	
book	Daisy	flag	had

hair	kitty	now	said
happy	know	nuts	sand
has			Santa Claus
have	left	of	says
he	let	oh	school
hear	like	old	see
hello	little	on	seen
help	lives	one	shall
hen	look	our	she
her	love	out	sing
here			sled
his	make	Paul	Snowball
holes	many	party	so
home	march	picture	soldier
hop	may	play	some
house	me	please	spider
how	meow	pretty	squirrels
hungry	milk		sunshine
hurrah	mother	rains	swing
	mouse	read	
I	Mr.	red	tell
if	Mrs.	ride	thank
in	must	right	Thanksgiving
is	my	Robert	that
it		robins	the
	name	rocking-horse	them
Johnny	nest	Rose	they
	new	run	think
kite	no	Ruth	this
kitten	not		three

to	umbrella	what	with
toad	under	where	woods
to-day	us	wherever	would
too		white	
Topsy	want	who	yellow
tree	was	whoa	yes
turkeys	water	why	you
two	we	will	your
	went	winter	

To avoid fine, this book should be returned on
or before the date last stamped below

CPSIA information can be obtained
at www.ICGtesting.com
Printed in the USA
LVHW022213170323
741893LV00032B/1383